"I hope that Muckross will be made a real garden of friendship, and that it will be the greatest playground in the world - there is not another in the world like it and I know them all."

Arthur Rose Vincent,
last owner and donor of the Muckross Estate to the Irish Nation

CONTENTS

	History	2	The Stream Garden
	Seeing Muckross Gardens	5	25 The Tree Ferns
	The Parterre and Terrace	6	26 The Boathouse Walk
	The Sunken Garden	7	28 The Lower Stream Garden
	The Heather Border	9	30 The Hydrangea Border
	The Lawns	10	31 The Arboretum
	The Rock Garden	13	32 The Old Woodland
	The Old Tennis Courts	17	34 The Camellia Walk
	Plan of the Gardens	18	37 Drumrower
	The Eastern Lawn	20	39 Facilities for Visitors

(C) Government of Ireland 1995

Published by the Stationery Office

ISBN 0-7076-1562-3

To be purchased through any Bookseller, or directly from
Government Publications Sales Office, Sun Alliance House, Molesworth Street, Dublin 2.

Written by Cormac Foley and Jim Larner
who wish to acknowledge the help and expertise of the horticultural staff of Killarney National Park.

Colour Photography by Con Brogan of the Office of Public Works unless otherwise stated.

Historical photographs from the Vincent archives kindly supplied
by A.W.B. Vincent of San Francisco, California.

Design by Creative Inputs

Separations by MasterPhoto Ltd

Printed by Mount Salus Press Ltd

MUCKROSS GARDENS AND ARBORETUM

To the south and west of Killarney, lies Killarney National Park, over 10,000 hectares in extent comprising the famous three lakes of Killarney and the mountains and woodlands which surround them. The nucleus of the National Park is the 4,300 hectare Bourn Vincent Memorial Park, formerly known as the Muckross Estate, which was presented to the Nation in 1932.

The best known area of the National Park to most visitors is the Muckross Demesne, of which the focal point is Muckross House and Gardens. The present House, successor to earlier mansions, was built in the Elizabethan style to the design of the Scottish architect, William Burn. Situated in a beautiful location close to the eastern shore of Muckross Lake, the House was completed in 1843. It now serves as the major visitor centre for the Park, and is jointly managed by the National Parks and Wildlife Service of the Office of Public Works and the Trustees of Muckross House (Killarney) Ltd.

The world-famous Muckross Gardens, 20 hectares in extent, adjoin Muckross House and contain many features which contribute to their beauty and interest. The design of the Gardens is informal and its large expanses of lawn within a woodland setting provide magnificent vistas of lake and mountain. The rock garden is an unusual feature, developed on a natural outcrop of fissured Carboniferous limestone. Close by, is a charming stream garden with attractive waterside plants.

The Gardens also contain fine specimens of *Cercidiphyllum japonicum, Cordyline australis, Dicksonia antarctica, Drimys winteri, Embothrium coccineum, Liriodendron tulipifera, Magnolia wilsonii, Malus sargentii, Nothofagus cunninghamii, Parrotia persica, Pinus sylvestris,* and several species of *Acer, Eucalyptus, Eucryphia* and *Sorbus*. The range of exotic and less hardy trees and shrubs is constantly being increased.

As an extension to the Gardens, an Arboretum has been established which contains a wide variety of less hardy trees. The screening woodlands include specimen trees of arboricultural interest. Notable among these are Giant Redwood, Monterey Pine, Lawson Cypress, and Yew, Oaks, Beech, Firs and Pines.

HISTORY

Gardens at Muckross were first described by William Ockenden in 1760. His description which is included in the book, "Observations of Modern Gardening" contains the following account. *"We began our view of these environs with Muckross Gardens, the property of Edward Herbert Esq.; they lie, or rather hang, upon The East End of the lake and consist of a most uncommon mixture of large rocks, shady valleys, and open lawns, extremely lively in their verdure."* However, the location of these gardens described by Ockenden is far from clear. In all probability, they adjoined the previous Muckross House in the area now known as the Monk's Wood, about 500 metres north of the present mansion.

The layout of the present Gardens was started in the 1840's by the Herbert family in conjunction with the building of the present Muckross House and many of the trees in the immediate vicinity of the House were planted at that time. These included Scots Pine, Silver Fir, Oaks and Beeches.

In 1855, it was announced that Queen Victoria was to visit Killarney in the autumn of 1861 and would stay at Muckross House as well as at Kenmare House, the residence of the Earl of Kenmare. Over the course of the next six years the entire Muckross Estate was groomed for the Royal arrival. Paths were opened up through the grounds and surrounding woods, viewing sites were prepared with platforms and seats. The Herberts instructed the gardeners to increase the number and variety of late-summer-flowering shrubs and flowers, and many of these were substantial plants by the time of Queen Victoria's visit.

In 1899 the Muckross Estate, which had been the family home of the Herberts for nearly 130 years, was sold to Lord Ardilaun, a member of the Guinness family who, in 1911, sold the property to Mr. William Bowers Bourn. Mr. Bourn, a wealthy Californian, gave the estate to his daughter, Maud, on her marriage to Mr. Arthur Vincent. Following the death of Maud in 1929, the 4,300 hectare Muckross Estate was given to the Nation and, in 1933, became Ireland's first National Park, known as the Bourn Vincent Memorial Park.

Between 1911 and 1932, during the years of Vincent ownership, over £110,000 was spent on various improvements to the estate, almost twice as much as Mr. Bourn had originally paid for it. Most of the developments of Muckross Gardens date from this time, and are due to the personal interest and involvement of Mr. Vincent. Plans for many developments were prepared

Before / After

Development of the Sunken Garden

Development of the Rock Garden

by the firm of R. Wallace and Co. of Colchester, England, Garden Architects, and these plans are conserved in the archives of the National Park. Many of the proposed developments never reached fruition including the development of a water garden based on a similar feature in Filoli, the family home of the Bourns in California. Fortunately, Mr. Vincent was also a keen photographer and recorded much of the work while it was in progress.

Improvements included a "parterre", formal terrace and sunken garden adjacent to the House. The rockery, on a naturally occurring outcrop of limestone, was also developed. This was cleared of scrub and planted with dwarf conifers and shrubs. Paths and steps were added to make the rockery more accessible. The southern end of the Gardens had been very wet and in order to drain this an existing stream bed was opened up to carry the drainage water into

Vegetable and fruit continued to be grown, but since there was no need for these at the House, they were sold to local residents. This practice was discontinued in the early 1960's and the emphasis was placed on the development of the fine collection of plants and shrubs which are present here today.

Muckross Lake. The stream banks were landscaped and planted with bog plants to form the Stream Garden as it exists today.

Greenhouses were erected in 1911 by W. Richardson and Co. of Darlington to supply grapes, nectarines and cut flowers for the House. Vegetables for the House were also cultivated in the Nursery Garden. Today, the greenhouses are used to grow bedding plants and to propagate trees and shrubs for the Gardens.

Following the departure of Mr. Vincent in 1932, and the take-over by the State, many of the management practices which had been introduced by Mr. Vincent continued.

As an extension to the Gardens, an Arboretum, nearly 15 hectares in extent, has been established. This collection of trees and shrubs was started in 1972, and complements the National Arboretum at the J. F. Kennedy Memorial Park in Co. Wexford. The wide variety of less hardy trees planted here include many from the Southern Hemisphere which flourish here in the mild climate of southwest Ireland.

In the mid-1980's a curvilinear conservatory of cast iron construction, dating from the 19th Century, was added in the nursery garden. This magnificent conservatory houses a rare collection of warm-temperate and tropical plants.

SEEING MUCKROSS GARDENS

The usual approach to Muckross Gardens is from the side of Muckross House overlooking Muckross Lake. However, there are other approaches, and consequently this guide refers to areas of particular interest within the Gardens rather than suggesting a specific route around the Gardens. These areas of interest are shown on the plan of the Gardens on p. 18-19. The major features of each area are outlined in the first paragraph with more detailed descriptions and plant listings in the following text.

THE PARTERRE AND TERRACE

The "parterre" and terraces which lie under the main windows of Muckross House overlooking Muckross Lake were laid out in the days of Vincent ownership. The "parterre" with its "crazy-paving" path of Killarney marble, is enclosed by a hedge containing Box *(Buxus)*, *Pernettya* and clipped Yew *(Taxus)*. Below the "parterre", a lower terrace of formal lawn is defined by a hedge mainly of cultivars of *Escallonia*.

A large bed of shrub roses (*Rosa rugosa*) was planted against the wall of the House by Mrs. Vincent. These are mainly of shades of red with some pink and white specimens and they exude a beautiful scent in July which permeates the main rooms of the House. Boston Ivy (*Parthenocissus sp.*), often mistakenly referred to as Virginia creeper, grows up the walls of the House and is best seen in Autumn when its leaves are of a striking scarlet hue.

THE SUNKEN GARDEN

The only formal landscape feature within Muckross Gardens, the Sunken Garden was designed by Wallace and Co. of Colchester, and laid out by Cashman's of Cork in 1915. The sunken garden is divided into two by a "crazy-paving" path. In the half closest to the House is a circular bed with an old plant of the pink-flowered Japanese Azalea (*Azalea obtusum* "Amoenum"). Four formal beds are planted with arrangements of Spring bedding which give a colour period from April to June and this is followed by Summer bedding, giving colour throughout the Summer months. The beds contain some standard roses to give height to the display.

A cast iron staircase rises to the window of the Ladies' boudoir and was used by the Head Gardener to deliver fresh cut flowers to the Lady of the House who supervised their arrangement. The room was used as Queen Victoria's sitting room during her visit to Muckross House in 1861.

Astilbe

Lobster Claw *(Clianthus puniceus)*

A large specimen of *Magnolia grandiflora*, is planted by the wall of the House. At its base is another climbing plant, the Lobster Claw (*Clianthus puniceus*), a native of New Zealand. Near the iron staircase is the Winter-Flowering Jasmine (*Jasminium nudiflorum*), while another species of Jasmine (*Jasminium stephanense*), grows in the corner on the wall of the House. Around the perimeter of the Sunken Garden the beds contain mixed herbaceous plants. The border closest to the Lake has a fine specimen of *Clematis montana* growing along the full length of the wall. This flowers right through April and May. Some of the herbaceous plants of note are groups of *Crocosmias* from South Africa and Canna lilies, which are tender plants, rarely cultivated out of doors. These show their fiery red blooms right through the Summer months. Other herbaceous plants present include *Aconitums*, Michaelmas Daisies, which bloom in the Autumn, as well as fine clumps of *Agapanthus* and of *Rodgersia aesculifolia*.

The border on the southern and eastern sides of the Sunken Garden contains *Astilbes*, Peonies, particularly the tender tree Peonies, Lupins, Gladioli, *Senecio, Schizostylis,* and *Romneya coulteri,* the white flowering plant known as the Californian Poppy. Two *Cypress* trees planted by the Herberts, form a feature at the southern end of the Sunken Garden.

C. FOLEY

THE HEATHER BORDER

Developed in the 1970's, the Heather Border is located on the lake side of a large clump of Rhododendron below the Sunken Garden end of the Terrace. It contains a range of heathers which give colour and interest all year round. Leading down from the Terrace to the Heather Border and standing on its own on an elevated embankment is a very large specimen of the Monterey Pine (*Pinus radiata*) from California. This grows more quickly in the humid conditions here in SW Ireland than it does in its native habitat of the Monterey Peninsula. This particular tree is approximately 120 years old.

The Heather Border contains many of the cultivars of the winter-flowering *Erica carnea* group. The summer-flowering heathers are mainly cultivars of the native heathers, *Erica tetralix, Erica cinerea* and *Calluna vulgaris* as well as cultivars of St. Dabeoc's Heath (*Daboecia cantabrica*). Some of the taller tree heathers of the Mediterranean, such as the cultivar *Erica mediterranea* "Brightness" are also featured here. Shrubs which thrive in the acidic peat are used for contrast. These include Japanese Azaleas and *Skimmia japonica* with its red berries in Winter. Dwarf conifers, in particular, *Thuya* "Rhinegold" with its spectacular golden foliage, the steel blue *Chamaecyparis* "Boulevard", and some taller cultivars of Lawson Cypress are also displayed.

THE LAWNS

The informality of the Muckross Lawns is perhaps one of the special charms of these famous Gardens. Expanses of lawn within a woodland setting, punctuated with fine clumps of mature hybrid Rhododendrons, frame magnificent vistas of lake and mountain. Scots Pines, planted by the Herberts around 1845, give scale to these vistas.

The Rhododendron clumps give a brilliant display of colour from April to July, with the peak of the colour in May and June. Colour shades range across the spectrum with many pinks and moderate reds. Many of these Rhododendrons were first developed in Victorian times and are varieties of *Rhododendron arboreum*, a species which was used as a parent for many new hybrids. Incorporated into the groups are mature hardy hybrids such as "Cynthia", "Britannia", "Pink Pearl","Purple Splendour"and "Sappho".

In the last fifty years newer cultivars such as "Mayday" and the double-flowered purple *Rhododendron* "Fastuosum Flore Pleno" have been added. Some of the early flowering varieties in the Gardens are "Louis Pasteur" and "Unknown Warrior". The Rhododendrons are accompanied by species and cultivars of Azalea and noteworthy among these are *Azalea obtusum* "Amoenum", *Azalea mollis* and Exbury hybrids.

Rhododendron Hardy Hybrids

The Scots Pines are a relatively long-lived species and were planted in the early 1840's around the time that Muckross House was built. Scots Pine (*Pinus sylvestris*) was native to Ireland but there is evidence to suggest that it became extinct in Ireland about 2,000 years ago. The provenance of the strain in Muckross Gardens is probably from Scotland. These are noted for their orange-coloured peeling bark in the upper reaches of the trees and their glaucous blue foliage. Scots Pines can live for up to 250 years, but as a long-term policy, some new groves and individual Scots Pines have been added in recent years to give a more varied age structure and a guarantee for the future. One such clump, directly in front of the Rock Garden was planted in the 1970's.

Azalea obtusum "Amoenum"

Scots Pines

Rhododendron "Cynthia"

Rhododendron "Purple Splendour"

THE ROCK GARDEN

The Rock Garden is an unusual feature developed on a natural outcrop of fissured Carboniferous limestone. A large erratic boulder of Old Red Sandstone, carried here by glacial action in the last Ice Age is perched on the limestone reef. Several pathways lead on and through the Rock Garden and vistas of the lawns interspersed with clumps of Rhododendrons and views of the surrounding Park lands and mountains open up from the top of the outcrop. The Rock Garden contains an extensive collection of dwarf and slow-growing conifers, prostrate shrubs, alpine perennials and a wide range of Spring bulbs.

Among the conifers growing on the Rock Garden are cultivars of *Thuya*, Pine, Juniper and Cypress, particularly of Lawson Cypress. Dwarf and prostrate shrubs include *Pittosporums, Hebes, Helianthus* and *Cotoneasters* as well as numerous cultivars of *Corokia* and *Leptospermums* from New Zealand and Australia, representatives of the Myrtle family from South America, *Yuccas* from central America, and the tree heath, *Erica arborea* from the Mediterranean. Autumn colour is enhanced by the presence of the Japanese Maples, the *Acer palmatum* group, in the company of Japanese Azaleas. One of the very best of the Maples is the variety "Senkaki", the Coral Bark Maple, with its beautiful pink bark and spectacular crimson Autumn leaf colour.

Erigeron in Flower

Larger scale trees form a backdrop to the Rock Garden and include specimens of the native Oak (*Quercus petraea*), Yew trees (*Taxus baccata*) and a grove of the native wild cherry (*Prunus avium*), with their spectacular white blossom in Spring. Other larger trees include the native *Arbutus unedo*, the Strawberry tree, some exceptionally fine conifers such as the Japanese White Pine (*Pinus parviflora*), numerous cultivars of Lawson Cypress including some fine examples of "Wisselii" and *Pinus mugo*. In more recent times, some larger examples of *Davidia*, Rhododendrons, including *Rhododendron augustinii,* and varieties of *Pieris* have been added.

About half way along the rock face, on the edge of the Lawn, is a specimen of the native Oak which is about 200 years old. Flanking the Oak are two excellent specimens of *Azalea obtusum* "Amoenum". Muckross Gardens probably contain some of the best examples of this magenta-flowered Azalea. Other plants on the front of the rockery include some of the dwarf conifers such as the golden form of Lawson Cypress "Stewartii" as well as the golden Thuya, *Thuya* Zebrina. Forming a dense mound on the rock, is the procumbent form of the Cedar of Lebanon, *Cedrus libani* "Sargentii", named after the great plant collector, Charles Sargent. Also appearing in numerous locations on the Rock Garden are the Bottle brushes, from Australia. These are of the *Callistemon* and *Melaleuca* families.

Oxalis and *Dianthus*

At the eastern end of the Rock Garden, a flight of sandstone steps leads up to a small platform with a stone table. This was used by the Vincents as a favourite spot for taking afternoon tea. To the right of the path approaching the steps is the Japanese Maple, known as *Acer palmatum* "Ribesifolium", so called because its leaves mimic *Ribes*, the flowering blackcurrant. Flanking the left of the path is a specimen of the purple leafed *Pittosporum tenuifolium*. This is one of the few purple leafed plants to retain its leaves all year round. On the right, perched directly on the steps, is the pendulous *Coprosma*, a native of the Australasian region, with another prostrate plant, the Rosemary, *Rosmarinus* "Severen Seas" adjacent to it. A plant which produces very red foliage in the winter months is from the Pacific region and is of the Bromelliad family, *Fasicularia pitcairniifolia*. This is a native of Pitcairn Island, the refuge of the mutineers from H.M.S. Bounty. In this corner also is a stand of what is known as the Sacred Bamboo, *Nandina domestica*. Although not strictly a bamboo, this plant is extensively cultivated in Japan, Korea and China. The mauve-flowered *Melaleuca gibosa* is a native of the Australasian region and another Australian plant here which is quite rare in cultivation is *Carmichaelia*, with its distinctive flattened branchlets. Forming a backdrop to all these plants in this corner is a very fine example of *Pittosporum* "Silver Queen".

Acer palmatum cultivar in Autumn.

Fasicularia pitcairniifolia

THE OLD TENNIS COURTS

Lawn tennis courts were laid out in this area during the years of Vincent ownership. These were re-landscaped in more recent times and the area now contains a collection of conifers. A trellis separates the Old Tennis Courts from the walled Nursery Garden. Good examples of climbing plants, including fruiting vines, grow on the trellis. In front of these is a fine hedge of *Escallonia* which flowers in profusion in early summer. This is interspersed with some oriental cherries which give good colour in April and May.

The re-landscaped Old Tennis Courts contain a collection of conifers including the Arizona Cypress (*Cupressus glabra*), the Oriental Spruce (*Picea orientalis*), and several cultivars of Lawson Cypress including the golden forms, "Lutea" and "Hillieri". Among the conifers, there are two specimens of the slow growing Paper-bark Maple (*Acer griseum*). This species is distinctive for its peeling rust-coloured bark. Because of the slowness of its growth, it is particularly suited to growing in garden lawns.

Separating the Old Tennis Courts from the rest of the Gardens is a low dry-stone wall, fronted by a border. Formerly known as the lavender border, it still contains some cultivars of lavender as well as many shrubs and sub-shrubs. These include *Colquhounia coccinea*, varieties of *Salvia*, cultivars of *Leptospermum*, *Corokia*, *Senecio* and *Potentilla*. Dwarf rhododendrons and Japanese Azaleas give a high colour impact to this border in the Spring.

Trellis with Fruiting Vine.

AREA:-
Muckross Gardens, 20 hectares.
Arboretum, 15 hectares.

LOCATION: -
9° 30'W longitude 52° 01'N latitude

GRID REFERENCE: -
V 9686.

CLIMATE: -
Oceanic, with mild winters and cool summers.
Annual rainfall:- 1253 mm. per year.
Number of rain days with more than 1 mm. of rain: - 223 days per year.
Mean air temperatures: -January, 5.8 degrees C
　　　　　　　　　　　　July, 15.2 degrees C

SOILS: -
Muckross Gardens are on Carboniferous Limestone with deeper soils of glacial drift from the Devonian Old Red Sandstone. These are moderately acidic.

1. Monterey Pine. *Pinus radiata*
2. Copper Beech. *Fagus sylvatica "Purpurea".*
3. *Gunnera manicata*
4. Caucasian Silver Fir. *Abies nordmanniana*
5. Western Hemlock Fir. *Tsuga heterophylla*
6. Giant Redwood. *Sequoiadendron giganteum*
7. *Rhododendron arboreum*
8. Montery Cypress. *Cupressus macrocarpa*
9. Monterey Pine. *Pinus radiata*
10. Sculpture — "Spirit of Oak".

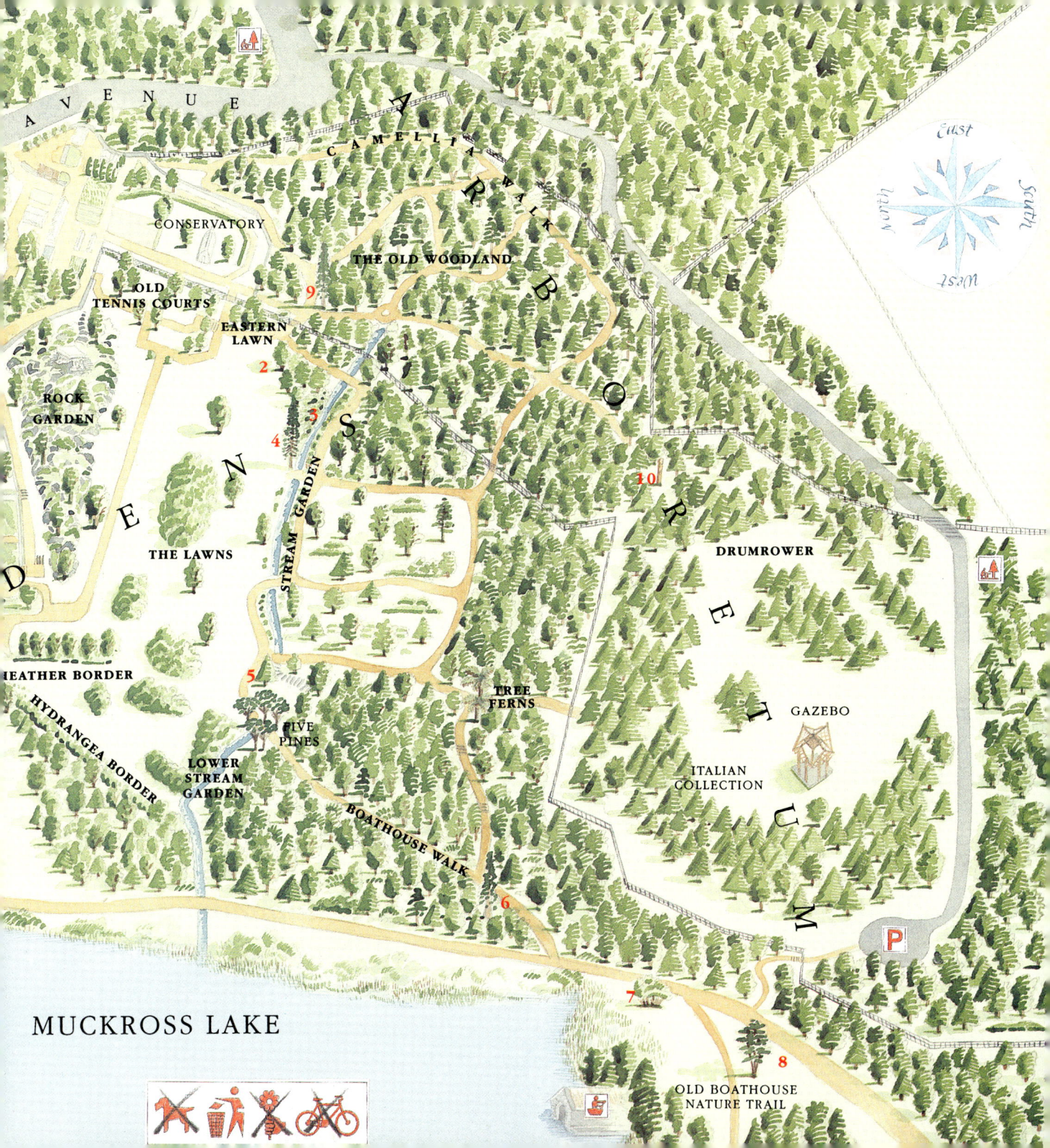

THE EASTERN LAWN

This area of the garden contains many interesting features and species in a gradual arrangement from the trellis enclosing the Walled Garden, through shrubberies to clumps of shrubs, and isolated specimens set in the Lawns.

By the side of the trellis gates into the walled Nursery Garden are two outstanding examples of the Japanese *Azalea obtusum* "Amoenum". These have beautiful magenta blossoms in April. Behind these, is a shrub border containing an example of the Empress Tree, *Paulownia*, which also flowers in Spring. Located in the Eastern Lawn is a mature Copper Beech beneath which is an extensive display of bulbs, with a wide range of Narcissi. On the other side of the path to the Copper Beech, is a young example of the Castlewellan Juniper (*Juniperus recurva* "Castlewellan"), a pendulous conifer with very fine feathery foliage. Two Mountain Ashes close to the path flower and fruit extremely well. These are *Sorbus aucuparia* "Joseph Rock", which has a very upright form with yellow berries and *Sorbus villmorinii*, more arching in form, with purple fruits which change colour to wine and then to pink and white.

By the stile into the Arboretum, a number of climbing plants have been trained onto the fence. Two of these are *Clematis montana*, and the Large-leafed Ivy, *Hedera colchica*. The latter is performing extremely well and has now climbed about 10 metres up the adjacent Oak tree. (From here you may choose to visit the Arboretum, the descriptive text for which is at p.31). The shrubbery includes specimens of *Mahonia japonica*, the winter-flowering Japanese Mahonia with its yellow flowers, specimens of the Star Magnolia (*Magnolia stellata*), which flowers on the bare twigs in Springtime and the tender evergreen shrub, *Pseudowintera colorata* with its mottled foliage. There are also some young specimens of the tree fern, *Dicksonia antarctica*, a native of Southern Australia and Tasmania. The large-leaved group of Rhododendrons on both sides of the path just north of the stream includes *Rhododendron sinogrande* with its gigantic leaves. This species comes from the Himalayas and grows very well here in the south west of Ireland. Adjacent to these large-leaved Rhododendrons is a specimen of a tender plant from Africa, *Myrsine africanum*, an evergreen shrub with aromatic myrtle-like leaves.

Sorbus vilmorinii

THE STREAM GARDEN

The Garden stream is fed by a natural spring which rises from the Carboniferous Limestone rock just to the east of the Gardens and flows in a northwesterly direction into Muckross Lake. The stream, which also serves to drain this lower end of the Gardens was cleared and its banks landscaped during the years of Vincent ownership. With its clear, clean waters and sandy substrate, the stream, particularly in the lower reaches, is often used by trout as a spawning bed. Attractive waterside plants in this charming Stream Garden include *Hosta fortunei, Melianthus major, Phormium tenax* "Veitchii", *Primula spp., Astilbe sp.,* and *Lysichiton americanus*, the American Skunk Cabbage.

Stream Garden General View

On the right of the path immediately across the stream, is a fine example of the large leaved evergreen Magnolia from China *Magnolia delivai*, with its large cream flowers. To the left of the path, the Dawn Redwood (*Metasequoia glyptostroboides*), with its tall pillar shape, is also from China. It is also known as the Living Fossil Tree, since it was thought to be extinct until re-discovered in China in 1941. Another Far-eastern species, is of the Mountain Ash family *Sorbus matsumurana*, with its red berries. Beneath this is a stand of deciduous azaleas, including "Honeysuckle", "Kathleen" and "Firefly" which flower in spring and in most cases are highly scented.

The Snow Gum (*Eucalyptus niphophila*), grows in its native habitat at altitude in the Snowy Mountains of Victoria and New South Wales in Australia. It is one of the smaller of the Eucalyptus species, suitable for small gardens and quite hardy as in the Snowy Mountains, it is often snow covered. Behind the Snow Gum the very large *Griselinia* from New Zealand, shows how this species would develop if it was not clipped as a hedge but allowed to grow freely. Adjacent to it are two unusual conifers, *Podocarpus acutifolius* with its light green foliage and a variegated form of the Chinese Juniper.

The Caucasian Fir (*Abies nordmaniana*), standing well over 30 metres in height, is perhaps the tallest conifer in the Gardens. The rhubarb-like plant beneath it is *Gunnera manicata*, a plant from South America with its gigantic leaves in Spring and Summer. Nearby, there is a free-standing specimen of a Myrtle (*Myrtus lechlerana*). This flowers profusely in the springtime and has highly scented cream flowers.

The stream border contains many species which thrive in moist conditions. These include New Zealand flax, a species which has become naturalised in parts of West Kerry, Arum Lilies, *Kniphofias* (Red-Hot Pokers), Day lilies, *Crinum* lilies, *Penstemons* and a large selection of *Hostas* which range

Deciduous Azalea Exbury Hybrid

from green-leafed varieties through variegated forms to blue leaved forms. *Astilbe* is another moisture-loving plant that thrives here. Other examples of waterside plants along the stream include Irises, *Bergenia,* and *Dierama.*

In the Lawn as the path crosses the stream, is a young example of the weeping form of the native Ash (*Fraxinus excelsior*), as well as another tree with Ash-like leaves, *Pterocarya fraxinifolia,* a Caucasian species belonging to the walnut family. By the side of the stream, near the stepping stones, are a number of water loving tree species. These include a specimen of *Nyssa sylvatica*, the Tupelo or Black Gum of North America, the Swamp Cypress (*Taxodium distichum*) from the southern United States and the red stemmed Westonbirt Dogwood (*Cornus alba* "Siberica"). There is also a good example on a drier site of the Tree Heath (*Erica arborea*), from the Mediterranean. Growing in the stream is the American Skunk Cabbage (*Lysichiton americanus).*

Gunnera manicata

Purple Loosestrife & Day Lilies

American Skunk Cabbage
(*Lysichiton americanus)*

THE TREE FERNS

To the south of the stream-side path a Carboniferous Limestone outcrop which, unlike the Rock Garden, was not cleared of its natural vegetation, provides a shaded environment and is ideal for shade loving species. At the base of the rock outcrop is a Western Hemlock (*Tsuga heterophylla*), a native of the west coast of America.

The path southwards leads passed deciduous Azaleas, particularly the yellow-flowered *Azalea mollis*, which give a spectacular and highly scented display in spring. Behind these is an example of *Parrotia persica,* a native of Persia. This small tree is rightly famed for the autumn colour of its foliage, which changes to a brilliant scarlet before fading to yellow. The South American aromatic shrub, *Drimys winteri,* known as Winterbark, reaches tree-like proportions in these milder climates. On the left of the path, a huge Rhododendron shrubbery contains many of the earlier forms of *Rhododendron arboreum* as well as many of the old Victorian hybrids such as "Pink Pearl", "Cynthia" and "Purple Splendour". Tree Ferns (*Dicksonia antarctica*) form part of the understorey of the temperate rain forests in Tasmania and Southern Australia. These conditions are simulated to a degree in the mild south west of Ireland, promoting the growth of these mature specimens. Behind the tree ferns, is a blue cultivar of Lawson Cypress, thought to be Lawson Cypress "Headfortii".

Azalea mollis

Tree ferns *(Dicksonia antartica)*

THE BOAT HOUSE WALK

The stream disappears underground for about 30 metres, before re-emerging again in the western end of the Gardens. The continuation of the path westwards leads to Dundag Bay on Muckross Lake passing shrub borders containing Azaleas, *Cornus, Magnolia, Desfontainea,* and *Eucryphia*. To view the plants along the Boat House Walk we suggest that you first concentrate on those along the southern (left) side of the path as you head for the Lake, viewing those on the northern side as you return to the Five Pines which you will see just ahead of you.

South of the path are three specimens of the Southern Beech (*Nothofagus cunninghamii*). This evergreen species is a native of the temperate rain forests of Tasmania, and is rarely found in cultivation. Beneath the Azaleas just ahead is a ground cover of the Winter Heliotrope (*Petasites fragrans*). Now naturalised in Ireland, the pink-purple flowers are highly scented particularly in the winter months. At this spot also, the flowering cherry is of the species *Prunus sargentii*, Sargent's Cherry.

Bordering the path are five Scots Pines. The orange colour of the peeling bark is particularly noticeable high up on the trunks, a particular feature of mature Scots Pines. Not unnaturally, this point is known as "The Five Pines". Just past the "Five Pines" is a group of *Skimmia japonica*, an evergreen shrub with red berries in winter. A specimen of *Fothergila monticola* has adjacent to it *Euonymus alatus,* noteworthy for its winged branchlets. The group of evergreens include some Japanese Cedars (*Cryptomaria japonica*) with their red peeling bark. These are accompanied by some South American species of *Eucryphia* and *Drimys winteri,* the Winterbark, which here is exceptional in size.

An example of the White-Flowering Crab Apple (*Malus sargentii*), is accompanied by *Viburnum tomantosum* with its horizontal growth habit and beautiful white flowers. These are set against a backdrop of Weeping Birch, and adjacent to it, the Tulip Tree (*Liriodendron tulipifera*), a native of the south eastern and mid-western United States.

The Five Pines

The very large tree on the northern side of the path at the end of the walk, is the Giant Redwood (*Sequoiadendron giganteum*), of the Sierra Nevada in California. This particular tree probably dates back to the introduction of this species into Ireland in the 1860's. The bark is very thick, soft and fibrous and can be punched with impunity. Because of this, the bark of this tree is often used by Treecreepers who burrow into it to roost, often in small colonies. From here you have a view of Dundag Bay with the reed beds and the two boat-houses. Just on the roadside, by the path to the boat-houses is a very large multi-stemmed specimen of *Rhododendron arboreum* which produces blood-red flowers in March and April.

Skimmia japonica

Returning towards the "Five Pines", the red lantern-like flowers are of the South American *Crinodendron hookerianum,* while behind it, one of the rarer conifers in the Gardens, the Formosa Cypress (*Chamaecyparis formosensis*). Some new additions to the plant collection include the Magnolia "Mark Jury", *Viburnum fragrans, Mahonia bealei,* the Californian Myrtle (*Myrica californica*), and various Acers.

Just before "the Five Pines" the shrub group contains, as well as many fine deciduous Azaleas, *Magnolia soulangiana, Hamamelis mollis, Cornus capitata* with its pink Autumn fruits, and a example of *Olearia zennorensis,* a hybrid Olearia which originated in Zennor in Cornwall.

The Old Boathouse

Rhododendron arboreum

THE LOWER STREAM GARDEN

From the Five Pines, the stream meanders through the lower grounds of the Gardens to enter the Muckross Lake in Dundag Bay. This area contains a number of water-side plants, including Bamboos, weeping forms of the Goat Willow, Ash and Pear as well as a specimen of Gingko, the Maidenhair tree of China. These plants are best viewed by walking along the grassy glade and crossing to the eastern (right hand) bank of the stream.

As you enter the grassy glade from the "Five Pines", on the far bank of the stream a group of Bamboos is thriving in the damp soils of the stream side. This clump includes a number of species and cultivars including some black-stemmed Bamboos. Two species of *Colletia* from South America, *Colletia cruciata*, mistakenly associated with Christ's Crown of Thorns and *Colletia armata*, are also present here. On the left of the glade, the Maidenhair Tree or Ginkgo (*Ginkgo biloba*), with its fan-shaped, bilobed leaves, is another living fossil. Now represented by this single species, Ginkgos were an important group of trees in the Jurrassic Period. A native of China, *Ginkgo biloba* is very slow growing and can live for over two hundred years. In some years, there may be little new growth at all. This specimen is quite tall which attests to its great age.

As the path crosses the stream, there is a clump of *Acanthus mollis,* also known as Bear's Britches, on the stream bank. Other water side plants include *Yuccas* and ornamental grasses. The wide variety of shrub material adjacent to the stream includes *Mahonias, Osmanthus, Eleagnus,* Cordylines and *Cortaderias* while the bulb display includes the Autumn crocus (*Colchicum),* many cultivars of *Iris,* and the Day Lily or *Hemerocallis.*

Gereral View with *Ginkgo biloba*

Trees with weeping branches are often associated with water side locations and weeping forms of the native Goat Willow (*Salix caprea),* known as the Kilmarnock Willow, because it was first discovered in Kilmarnock in Scotland and a specimen of the Weeping Pear (*Pyrus communis pendula*), with its silver leaves grow here. Other plants by the stream are *Corokia buddleiioides* and *Corokia virgata* which are natives of New Zealand. There are also many species of *Pittosporum* including the very small-leaved *Pittosporum bicolor*.

Opposite the large specimen of Oak on the western bank of the stream, there is an unusual freak of botany, a graft hybrid of the Medlar Pear and the Hawthorn. Other trees in this location include the Bird Cherry (*Prunus padus),* the Pocket Handkerchief Tree (*Davidia involucrata*), from China, a Weeping Ash and another fine *Metasequoia*. Shrubs include some more examples of *Mahonia* including the species *Mahonia lomarifolia,* a native of China, while another Far Eastern species is the Bamboo, *Sassa palmata* and its variegated form, *Sassa palmata* "Variegata".

Nerine Lilies

Mahonia lomarifolia

THE HYDRANGEA BORDER

A long wavy-edged border of Hydrangeas leads you back up towards Muckross House. This includes a wide variety of Hydrangeas which give good flowering value in the later Summer months. As you walk back towards the House, you will see again how the Scots Pines give scale to the Lawns.

The numerous colour forms of Hydrangea along the border include lacecap and hortensia types as well as a number of individual species. The predominant colour is blue since the soil is relatively acidic. Some of the interesting trees behind the Hydrangeas, are the Autumn Cherry (*Prunus subhirtella* "Autumnalis"), cultivars of *Eucalyptus* and the Maples "Prinz Handjery" and "Brilliantissimum".

At the Muckross House end of the Hydrangea Border, a new shrub grouping contains a specimen of the Chilean holly (*Desfontainea spinosa*), a beautiful golden form of the Mexican Orange Blossom (*Choisya ternata*), the Tree of Heaven (*Ailanthus altissima*), several *Mahonias*, a number of *Sorbus* varieties and a variegated form of the native holly (*Ilex aquifolium*).

Hydrangea (Hortensia type)

Chilean holly *(Desfontainea spinosa)*

THE ARBORETUM

As an extension to the Gardens, an Arboretum, nearly 15 hectares in extent, was established in 1972. This complements the National Arboretum at the J. F. Kennedy Memorial Park in Co. Wexford. It contains a wide variety of less hardy trees, many from the Southern Hemisphere, which flourish here in the mild climate of southwest Ireland. Enclosed within a two metre high deer-proof fence, the Arboretum is in two parts; a shaded area, located in Old Woodland and an open site in the adjacent field known as Drumrower. Drumrower can also be reached by car from the main drive to Muckross House but please park in the areas provided and not on the roadside.

THE OLD WOODLAND

The canopy of the old woodland favours a wide range of tender plants which thrive in the dappled shade and shelter provided by the large native Oaks (*Quercus petraea*), Scots Pines (*Pinus sylvestris*), Monterey Pines (*Pinus radiata*), and Birch (*Betula pubescens*). Hollies, both green and variegated, *Acers, Hoheris, Clethras* and Southern Beeches planted here all thrive in the acid soil and shady conditions. This area now contains one of Ireland's premier collections of Camellias with nearly 100 different varieties planted here since 1980. Large groups of Exbury Azaleas have also been established.

The following description is written for the visitor who approaches the Arboretum from the direction of the Eastern Lawn. Twenty metres along the path to the left, inside the ornamental gate of the Arboretum, is a fine specimen of *Eucalyptus cordata*, with its glaucous blue leaves. This retains its sessile foliage throughout its life. A walk to the highest point of the Old Woodland gives an overview of the walled Nursery Garden and an appreciation of the varied species planted in the Arboretum. On the right of the path leading to the high point is an enormous Monterey Pine (*Pinus radiata*), one of the largest examples of this Californian species in the country. On the left of the path is an excellent example of *Drimys winteri* with a glaucous undersurface to the large evergreen leaves. Adjacent to this are two specimens of *Podocarpus toatara*, a native of New Zealand. The variegated *Pittosporum eugenoides* "Variegatum" is alongside. Proceeding up the hill, look out for a specimen of the Japanese

White Pine on the left of the path. This particular specimen is of the blue form, *Pinus parviflora* "Glauca" and is growing in the company of a collection of Rhododendrons and Azaleas. Located in the same area is a young example of *Sorbus headlundii,* a tender species, with large soft leaves. Ascending further, on both sides of the path are large plantings of species and hybrid Rhododendrons including *Rhododendron yakushimanum*, a native of Japan, with many of its named hybrid forms.

The building of the Nursery Garden was contemporaneous with the building of Muckross House and therefore dates to the middle years of the 1840's. It was used from then until the 1960's for the production of fruit and vegetables. Today, this walled garden is used as a nursery area, raising new and replacement plants for the Gardens. The curvilinear Conservatory dates to the last century and was formerly located in the Kenmare Estate, the other large estate of the Killarney Valley, which is now incorporated into the National Park. The Conservatory contains a collection of rare plants from warm-temperate parts of the world which could not be cultivated in the open.

Walled Garden with Conservatory

THE CAMELLIA WALK

With the right balance of dappled shade, suitable protection from the bright morning sun, and shelter, this area is ideal for the growing of Camellias. These are intermixed with individual specimens of a wide range of other tender plants including numerous species of *Sorbus, Ilex, Pieris,* and *Cornus*.

Camellia japonica cultivar

Camellias flower from very early Spring, many commencing early in January in mild winters with their flowering season extending to April or May. The individual varieties are grown in groups with over 100 varieties under cultivation. They range in colour from reds and pinks to whites, yellows and creams; their blossoms set off against their glossy dark green leaves. The varieties grown are of both the *Camellia japonica* and the *Camellia williamsii* types.

To the right of the path is a fine stand of large-leaved Rhododendrons from the

Camellia williamsii hybrids

Himalayas. These are represented by mature and young plants of *Rhododendron sinogrande* and *Rhododendron macabeanum*. Two young examples of another large-leaved Rhododendron, the much rarer *Rhododendron protistum,* were transferred to the Arboretum from the Gardens at Glenveagh National Park in 1986. These, in time, will reach large tree proportions.

Rhododendron sinogrande

On the reef of Carboniferous limestone an example of natural woodland has been included in the Arboretum displaying a group of the native Yew (*Taxus baccata).* Killarney is famed for its native Yew woodland and the largest area of this is on the Muckross Peninsula, just west of Muckross House. In the heavy shade cast by these trees is a ground cover of the introduced species, *Vinca minor,* the Lesser Periwinkle, as well as native species such as ivy and holly which thrive in the dense shade. In this area, too, are some large specimens of the native Sessile Oak (*Quercus petraea*) with mosses, liverworts and the Oak Fern or Polypody growing as epiphytes on their trunks and branches. Woodrush (*Luzula sylvatica*), a common species of the ground layer of Oak woods is also growing in abundance.

At the bottom of the incline, a late flowering species of Rhododendron, *Rhododendron auriculatum,* is present which, with its large white blossoms, flowers right into July. Behind this is an example of the Indian Chestnut (*Aesculus indica),* in the company of some species Magnolias. Adjacent to the path are some examples of *Hoherias,* natives of New Zealand. These ornamental trees can only survive in Ireland in these milder south western counties.

Epiphytes on Oak branches

Various species and varieties of *Photinia, Mahonia,* and numerous *Corokias* have been planted here. To the right of the path, some rare conifer species have been planted including *Picea spinulosa, Picea brachytyla, Picea omorika,* and *Picea breweriana,* which are all members of the Spruce family, as well as numerous species of Pine including *Pinus thunbergii* (the Japanese Black Pine) and *Cupressus goveniana* from California.

Magnolia cambelli

The area at the crossroads, where the sign indicates the path to the Drumrower section of the Arboretum, contains many rare specimens including the tender *Atherosperma moschatum,* an Australasian species which is thriving in this location, as well as the pink flowered form of the native Arbutus (*Arbutus unedo* "Rubra"). Young specimens of the Tree Fern (*Dicksonia antarctica),* planted in 1972 as sporelings have thrived in the shade and shelter provided under the woodland canopy. Also located in this area is an outstanding specimen of *Azara dentata* from Chile as well as the Chilean Hazel (*Gevuina avellana).* A good example of *Magnolia cambelli* is close by.

Departing from the Old Woodland area of the Arboretum, the passage way that leads into Drumrower contains many unusual specimens. The Incense Cedar (*Calocedrus decurrens)* is located here as is a rapidly growing example of *Cupressus macrocarpa* "Goldcrest". *Daphniphyllum humile,* a plant rare in cultivation and found only in the mildest areas, is growing behind this conifer. The white-flowered *Crinodendron patagua,* from Patagonia, at the southern tip of South America, is growing on the left of the path. This is less well-known than the more common red-flowered species, *Crinodendron hookerianum.* A stand of the Southern Beech, (*Nothofagus antarctica),* a native of South America, completes the collection.

DRUMROWER

With its deep soils of glacial till, growth of the trees planted in Drumrower has been very rapid. In 1973, Lawson Cypress, Japanese Larch, Scots Pine, various mixed conifers, Birch and Poplar were planted as a shelter matrix. Within this, collections of *Acers, Betulas, Cercidiphyllums, Pittosporums* and *Podocarpus* and trees of the Southern Hemisphere have been established. Many of the matrix trees have now been removed but some still remain to give shelter to the less hardy trees. A Gazebo provides a focal point to Drumrower and the main grass ride leads up to this. While many may choose to follow the path up to the Gazebo, there is much more to see for those who choose to wander around the family groups of trees, all of which are labelled.

In this area conifers in particular have profited from the deep soil and the mild conditions of the south west. Species include the Dawn Redwood (*Metasequoia glyptostroboides*), as well as the Noble Fir (*Abies nobilis*) and the giant Silver Fir (*Abies grandis*), which are both species from the Pacific northwest of America.

A collection of Maple species including a number of the Snake-bark Maples and species and cultivars of Birch are also planted here. These include *Betula jacquemontii, Betula utilis, Betula nigra, Betula papyrifera, Betula costata* and *Betula albosinensis*. Southern Hemisphere species include the Podocarps, many of them from New Zealand, Southern Beeches including *Nothofagus procera* and *Nothofagus obliqua* from South America, and various species of *Eucalyptus* from Australia.

The "Spirit of Oak" Sculpture

Winter cones on *Thuya* cultivar

Autumn colour of *Cornus kousa*

The Gazebo

Located at the highest point of the Arboretum, a Gazebo, made of Muckross - grown Larch, was erected in 1989 and this provides a focal point with fine views over the Arboretum and a panorama of the mountains beyond. To the east is Mangerton Mountain and to the south, the hump back of Torc Mountain. Westward the view is of the Purple mountain and MacGillycuddy's Reeks. Growing on the trellis are a number of climbers including *Vitis coignetiae, Wisteria* and various species of Honeysuckle (*Lonicera spp.*).

The Italian Collection

The path back to the main area of the Gardens is via a stile located in the Deer fence which will return you to the Tree Ferns. (p. 25). Near to the Gazebo is a grove of Italian trees dedicated to the memory of Monsignor Hugh O'Flaherty, a native of Killarney and better known as the "Scarlet Pimpernel" of the Vatican. Monsignor O'Flaherty was in the Vatican Diplomatic Service during World War II and was able, at great risk to himself, to assist Allied Airmen and escaped prisoners of war to evade capture by the Germans in Rome after the Allied invasion of Italy. The collection was dedicated to his memory by his nephew, Judge Hugh O'Flaherty, Justice of the Supreme Court on 11th June 1994. The grove includes specimens of the Italian Cypress (*Cupressus sempervirens*), the Holm Oak (*Quercus ilex*), Stone Pine (*Pinus pinea*), and the Mediterranean Palm (*Chamaerops humilis*).